The Purpose Of Life

The Manifesto of the Fort Hood Shooter

TERRORIST?

Nidal Hasan

with

Andrew McMurphy

 I do not support Nidal Hasan in any way, he gets no money from this book. I do not agree with the person he is and this book is for education only, it is not to incite violence or encourage people to be like him. If you feel like you admire him, I suggest you seek help. This book is not to recruit you into committing any crime and if you feel the urge to break the law talk to someone.

Table of Contents

Warning

What Nidal Hasan was wrong and no one should ever harm another person. That behavior is disgusting if you feel the need to hurt yourself or others call 911 and seek help. You may also call 988 Suicide & Crisis Lifeline 24 hours a day. Do not ever hurt yourself or others.

This book may upset you or others and this book is for education purposes only! It's to understanded Nidal Hasan so, maybe we can see the signs next time. To see the signs maybe we could prevent this from ever happening again.

Being a Muslim in America is not a crime and nor should anyone hate a Muslim because someone who commits a crime is one. Hating another for their religion is not the way. Being a Muslim does not make you a terrorist don't judge others and have an open mind while reading this book. Knowing the signs of an extremists may help save lives.

Do your part in keeping America safe by knowing the signs of an extremist.

About Nidal Hasan

This chapter uses material from the Wikipedia article
https://en.wikipedia.org/wiki/Nidal_Hasan

Nidal Malik Hasan born September 8th, 1970 is a former Army major convicted of killing 13 people and injuring more than 30 others in the Fort Hood mass shooting on November 5th, 2009. Hasan was an Army Medical Corps psychiatrist. He admitted to the shootings at his court-martial in August 2013. A jury panel of 13 officers convicted him of 13 counts of premeditated murder, 32 counts of attempted murder, and unanimously recommended he be dismissed from the service and sentenced to death. Hasan is incarcerated at the United States Disciplinary Barracks at Fort Leavenworth in Kansas awaiting execution.

During the six years Hasan was a medical intern and resident at the Walter Reed Army Medical Center, colleagues and superiors were concerned about his job performance and comments. Hasan was not married at the time, and was described as socially isolated, stressed by his work with soldiers, and upset about their accounts of warfare. Two days before the shooting, less than a month before he was due to deploy to Afghanistan, Hasan gave away many of his belongings to a neighbor.

Prior to the shooting, Hasan expressed critical views described by colleagues as "anti-American". An investigation conducted by the Federal Bureau of Investigation (FBI) concluded his emails with the late Imam Anwar al-Awlaki were related to his authorized professional research and he was not a threat. The FBI, Department of Defense (DoD) and U.S. Senate all conducted investigations after the shootings. The DoD classified the events as "workplace violence", pending prosecution of Hasan in a court-martial. The Senate released a report describing the mass shooting as "the worst terrorist attack on U.S. soil since September 11, 2001". The decision by the Army not to charge Hasan with terrorism is controversial.

Nidal Hasan was born in Arlington County, Virginia at Virginia Hospital Center to American parents of Palestinian descent; they immigrated years earlier from al-Bireh, a city in the West Bank near Jerusalem. Raised in the Muslim faith with his two younger brothers, he attended Wakefield High School in Arlington for his freshman year in 1985. His family moved to Roanoke in 1986, to join his father who moved to the city a year prior to set up what would become a number of successful family-owned businesses which included a market, restaurant, and olive bar.

He attended William Fleming High School in Roanoke, Virginia graduating from high school in 1988. Their father died in 1998 at the age of 51. Their mother, known as Nora by the community, died in 2001 at the age of 49. As adults, one brother continues to live in Virginia while the other moved to Palestine. Nidal is believed to have two sons.

On November 5th, 2009, Hasan reportedly shouted "Allahu Akbar!" (the phrase means "God is great"), and opened fire on armed forces in the Soldier Readiness Center of Fort Hood, located in Killeen, Texas, killing thirteen people and wounding over thirty others in the worst shooting against armed forces on an American military base.

Department of the Army police officer Kimberly D. Munley encountered Hasan exiting the building. Munley and Hasan exchanged shots before Munley was shot in the leg twice. Department of the Army police officer Mark Todd shot Hasan several times. Todd kicked the pistol out of Hasan's hand, then cuffed Hasan. The attack lasted about ten minutes.

To save his life, Hasan was hospitalized in the intensive care unit at Brooke Army Medical Center at Fort Sam Houston in San Antonio, Texas. His condition was described as "stable". News reports on November 7th, 2009, indicated he was in a coma. On November 9th, hospital spokesperson Dewey Mitchell announced Hasan re-gained consciousness, and was able to talk since he was removed from a ventilator on November 7th.

On November 13th, Hasan's attorney, John Galligan, announced Hasan was paralyzed from the waist down from the bullet wounds to his spine, and would likely never walk. In mid-December, Galligan indicated Hasan was moved from intensive care to a private hospital room. Galligan said doctors said Hasan would need at least two months in the hospital to learn "to care for himself".

On August 23rd, 2013, the military jury consisting of nine colonels, three lieutenant colonels, and one major convicted Hasan of all charges, making him eligible for the death penalty. Those deliberations began on August 26rd, 2013. By August 27th, the thirteen-member panel of jurors heard testimony from twenty-four victims and family members of those wounded and killed during the 2009 Fort Hood attacks against American armed forces. Throughout the proceedings, Hasan declined to speak in his defense or question any of the witnesses. He also did not provide any material explaining his decision to not mount a defense throughout the trial and sentencing. At the end, Hasan, acting as his attorney, told jurors the defense rested his case. Judge Tara Osborn accepted Hasan's decision. In his final statement, lead prosecutor Colonel Mike Mulligan said Hasan can never be a martyr because he has nothing to give ... Do not be misled; do not be confused; do not be fooled. He is not giving his life. We are taking his life. This is not his gift to God, it's his debt to society. He will not now and will not ever be a martyr.

The jurors re-convened to decide sentencing. On August 28th, 2013, the jurors recommended Hasan be sentenced to death. The panel also recommended Hasan forfeit his military pay and be dismissed from the Army, a separation for officers carrying the same consequences as a dishonorable discharge. Due to mandatory appeals and the military's historical reluctance to execute convicts, any execution is years away.

On August 28th, 2014, Hasan's attorney said Hasan wrote to Abu Bakr al-Baghdadi, then head of the Islamic State of Iraq and the Levant (ISIL). In the letter, Hasan requested to be made a citizen of the Islamic State, and included his signature and the abbreviation SOA (Soldier of Allah).

Understanding what the Holy Qurán actually says instead of what some may want it to say by carefully referencing the Quranic verses and placing them in the context they were revealed.

Towards Understanding Islam

MANS DUTY TO HIS CREATOR and THE PURPOSE OF LIFE

by

SoA

"They intend to put out the Light of Allāh (swt) with their mouths; but Allāh (swt) declines but to make full His (swt) Light, even though the disbelievers hate it-[9:32]."

Preface

Although my lawyer(s) will hand this work to the Convening Authority, I hope it also reaches the hands of all those that were effected by my actions. My intention is not to offend anyone, but to try to accurately convey to them my understanding of Islam and how I view the world; man's duty to his Creator; the purpose of life. I put much effort in trying to accurately convey the teachings of the Qurán by referencing the supporting Quranic verses and using those verses in the historical context they were understood. This work should also help in understanding the mindset of the mujahadeen (Holy Warriors) around the world. Their should be no doubt in anyone's mind that my actions were in the defense of Islam. Only All-Mighty God will decide whether He will accept my efforts as a Holy-Warrior or rebuke me for misunderstanding His Holy Book (Qurán). In the latter, I hope for God's forgiveness. I will spend the remainder of my life, God willing, trying to improve myself in the sight of my Lord. I hope to be a resident of Paradise and will continue to pray that others will try to attain the same (i.e. accept Islam). Reading this, I hope, will help. But, most are averse to the truth.

Disclaimer

1. This work (and all others that quote the Qurán) assumes that our Islamic forefathers accurately preserved the Qurán from the lips of our noble Prophet as revealed by All-Mighty God. So when I or other Muslim say: "God says this in the Qurán", it should be with that understanding. Although Islamic scholars debate whether the Quran we use today is 100% (exactly) as it was revealed from the mother book (al-Lawh al-Mahfuz) it is without doubt the best source of guidance for the God-fearing. May All-Mighty Allāh forgive us for any mistakes in trying to convey the truth on God's behalf.

2. Translations of the Quran into english or any other language/languages are really interpretations of the meanings of the Qurán. This is done to make it easier for non-arabic speakers to understand. This is important to understand because there will be differences in opinions on how to word a translation into a different language. Some tend to take more liberty than others in doing so. Since I am neither fluent in arabic nor an Islamic scholar, I depended heavily on such translations. So, be careful; I only want the good that comes from this work. The words of man should never override the words of God.

(3) I'm a sincere Muslim trying to accurately report the message of the Qurán in a simple and straight forward manner. Since I'm not an Islamic scholar, I cited the verses I used and tried to place them in the historical context they were used with few exceptions. But even then the reader should come to the same logical conclusion. I leave it to the responsibility of the reader to report any errors in this work so they are not propagated. My goal is to attain Heaven and help other to do so also; and not lead others to Hell.

(4) I'm no expert in Christianity but have referenced biblical verses with the hope that the followers of the Bible will appreciate that the same God that sent Jesus with the Gospel also sent Muhammad with the Qurán. Any verse that compromises monotheism must be rejected outright. All verses should be read through the lens of strict monotheism. Christians need to understand the origins of the Bible and realize it's weaknesses. Christians also need to realize that their forefathers took the letters of a man and made those letters the word of God and a big part of the Bible. The words attributed to Paul have huge errors and thus mix truth with falsehood. The Qurán was sent to reject the false hood.

The Start of My Journey

I sat in distress. My beloved mother was dying you see. I cried out to my Lord! Let this be over please! She was surrounded by loved ones. They loved her dear. Become religious for her sake, one of them screamed. I thought for a moment. I thought in silence. I won't become religious for mom. That makes no sense. I will become religious for All-Mighty God. That makes total sense. My mother can no longer hear me. But not All-Mighty God. So my journey began. I made a pact. I would be steadfast in prayer. I would stay on track. I had no idea. This religious journey was severe. I would learn the Purpose of Life. It wasn't the American Dream. That all changed you see. I was now trying to be obedient to the All-Mighty Lord of all the beings.

* note: each chapter may start with a poem or personal note.

Chapter 1

The Purpose of Life: Why Were We Created?

And when your Lord said to the Angels: "I (God) am going to set in the earth a successor"; they (the angels) said: Will you set therein such as will make trouble in there and will shed blood, while we (the angels) proclaim sanctity with Your praise and declare Your Holiness? He (God) said: "Verily I know what you do not Know" — [2:30].

"Do deeds! Allāh will see your deeds, and His Messenger and the believers; and you will be brought back to the [All]-knower of the unseen and the seen—[9:105].

The Purpose of Life

Why Were We Created?

All-Mighty God makes clear that mankind was created for a purpose. Our Lord asks and declares:

> O man, what has deluded you about your Lord the Beneficient—[82:06]?

> Does man think he will be left to no purpose—[75:36]?

> Do you think that We had but created you in vain and that you will not be brought back to Us—[23:115]?

> We have not created the heaven and earth and all that is between them for fun—[38:27; 21:16; 44:38; 15:85].

The Holy Qurán tells mankind that they were created to worship only Allāh:

> And I (Allāh) created not the Jinn and mankind but

that they should worship
Me[swt]—[51:56].

Prophet Muhammad[saws], who All-Mighty God[swt] describes as a good example for those who look forward to meeting their Lord[swt]—[33:21], was commanded to tell the people:

Verily my prayers, my sacrifice,
my living and my dying are for
Allah[swt] the Lord[swt] of all beings—[6:162;
See also 21:73].

Our Most-Gracious Lord[swt] further elaborates by saying He[swt] created life, death, the Heavens, the earth, and all of its adornments to test us to see who of us are best in deed—[67:02; 11:07; 18:07; 76:02; See also 5:48; 21:35; 10:14; 23:30; 45:22]; and will reward those who believe for those good deeds out of His[swt] Grace—[30:45; 4:173; 35:29-30; 24:38; See also 18:02; 76:22; 3:57; 40:40; 29:58; 34:37; 37:136; 32:19; 13:29; 16:111; 19:96; 20:112; 30:15; 31:08; 39:70; 45:30; 47:12; 32:17; 20:75; 64:17; 21:94; 16:97; 10:04]. All-Mighty God[swt] says:

Blessed is He[swt] in Whose Hand

> is the dominion; and He[swt] is over everything Omnipotent. He[swt] Who created death and life that He[swt] might test you as to who of you is the best in deed. And He[swt] is the Mighty, the Forgiving—[67:01-02; see also 18:07; 11:07; 45:22; 18:07, 9:105]. That He[swt] may reward those who believe and do the good deeds out of His[swt] Grace. Verily, He[swt] does not like the unbelievers—[30:45].

Getting Close to God[swt] and Entering Heaven

Our Beautiful Lord[swt] tells us that it is the performance of these good deeds that brings the believers close to Him[swt]—[9:99; 34:37]; and that through these good deeds (i.e. like obeying God's[swt] commandments) the believers can obtain His[swt] Love—[19:96; 3:31], Mercy—[45:30; 9:99], and Forgiveness—[3:134-136].

> Say (O Muhammad[saws] to mankind): If you Love Allah[swt] then follow me (i.e. accept Islam), Allah[swt] will love you and forgive you of your sins. And Allah[swt] is Forgiving, Merciful. Say: "Obey Allah[swt] and the Messenger[saws]". But if

they turn away, then Allāh
does not like the disbelievers
—[3:31-32];[Compare to Bible—John 8:42; 16:27]
Verily those who believe and do
the good deeds there will set
for them the [Most]-Merciful
(i.e. Allāh) love—[19:96].

This command of doing good deeds isn't new. This same message was given to Abrāham, Issāc, and Jacōb:

And Wē gifted to him
(Abrāham) Ishāq (Issāc),
and Ya'qūb (Jacōb) in addition;
and all Wē made righteous.
And Wē made them leaders
giving guidance by Oūr command;
and Wē communicated to
them the doing of good deeds
and performance of prayers
and payment of zakah (charity).
And they were of Ūs worshippers
—[21:72-73];[See also 23:51]

Similarly Mōsés was told:

> "Verily I am Allāh. There is no god but I. So worship Mē and establish the prayer for My remembrance. Verily the Hour is coming. <u>I would rather keep it secret, so that requited may be every individual for what it strives</u>—[20:14-15].

All-Mighty Gōd tells us that every single good and bad deed is recorded; and if the weight of one's good deeds isn't overwhelmed by the weight of one's bad deeds then that person shall enter Heaven—[99:06-8; 101:6-11; 2:81; 7:8-9; 23:102-104; 18:49; 17:13-14; 3:30]:

> That Day (i.e. Day of Judgement) man will come out in different groups in order to be shown their deeds. So whoever does the weight of atom in good shall see it. And whoever does the weight of an atom in evil shall see it—[99:06-08; 18:49; 3:30]. So as to the one of whom heavy will be the scales (of good deeds), he will be in a life very pleasant. And as to the one of whom light will become his scales (of good deeds as compared

to bad deeds), his abode will be the Abyss. And what will inform you what it is? It is a fire extremely hot—[101:06-11].
O yes; whoever earns a sin and there encircle him his sins, such ones will be the inmates of the fire; they in there will abide for ever—[2:81].

And every man, We[swt] have attached to him his deeds in his neck; and We[swt] shall produce to him on the Day of Resurrection a book he will encounter unfolded." Read your book; you yourself are sufficient today against you as account taker"—[17:13-14].
And you will see every people down on their knees. Every people will be called to their book. Today you will be requited for what you used to do—[45:28].

Reward and Ranks in Heaven and Hell

All-Mighty God[swt] mentions the different ranks or degrees of honor achieved by striving for these good deeds with due effort:

> And whoever desires the Hereafter and strives for it, with the necessary effort due for it while he is a believer, then such are the ones whose striving will be appreciated... [and] see how We[SWT] prefer one above another (in this world—[43:32; 16:71; 6:165; 4:32; 2:253; 17:55; 17:20; 6:86; 6:83; 11:3]) and verily, the Hereafter will be greater in degrees and greater in preferment—[17:19-21; See also 46:19; 3:163; 34:37; 20:75; 35:32; 6:132; 52:20; 64:17].

> Believers are those who, if mention is made of Allah[SWT], awe struck are their hearts; and if recited unto them are His[SWT] revelations, these increase them in faith; and on their Lord[SWT] they rely—who properly perform the prayers; and out of what We[SWT] provide, they spend. Such are the ones who are believers in truth. They will have ranks near their Lord[SWT] and forgiveness and a generous provision—[8:02-04; See also 10:02].

This notion of God[SWT] rewarding the believers who diligently seek Him[SWT] should be familiar to the Christians for their own scriptures say:

> "But without faith it is impossible to please Him[SWT] (God[SWT]): for he that cometh to God[SWT] must believe that He[SWT] is, and that He[SWT] is a rewarder of them that diligently seek Him[SWT]" – [Hebrews 11:6; See Appendix].

* Although Paul falsely believed Jesus was crucified for our sins, etc., he is accurate about God being the Rewarder.

Obviously its by God's Grace and Mercy that we are rewarded with Heaven, etc., but God[SWT] expects an effort. The Bible says:

> ... faith without works is dead... by works man is justified, and not by faith only... For as the body without the spirit is dead, so faith without works is dead – [James 2:20-26];

[See also John 5:29; James 2:14-26].

Although the rank All-Mighty God gives (some over others in things like livelihood – [43:32; 16:71] in this world) can be viewed as an honor, it's also part of the test to see what one does with this honor – [6:165; 4:32; 6:83; 17:70; see also 2:253; 6:26; 17:55; 28:76-82] and can be taken away at any time – [67:15-18; 2:155]. The believers should be aware of this and thus use their worldly rankings as a means to achieve a high rank in the Hereafter. Even the Prophets are ranked – [2:253; 6:86; 17:55] and seek a rank closest to All-Mighty God – [17:57; see also 17:79]. Everyone will have ranks according to their deeds. The Holy Qurán says:

> And for everyone will be ranks according to what they did and that He (God) might repay fully for their deeds; and they will not be wronged – [46:19; see also 16:11 6:132].
>
> Is then the one who pursues Allāh's pleasure like the one who incurs the wrath of Allāh? And his habitation is hell, and bad is the destination. They are of ranks in the sight of Allāh. And Allāh is [All-] Seeing of what they do – [3:162-163; see also 28:76-82].
>
> (See also Bible – John 5:29)

* Special Note: The Qur'an mentions 3 types of men. Which fits closest to you?

(A) Those who only ask for the good things of the world and strive accordingly - [2:200]; [11:15-16]

(B) Those who ask God (swt) for the good things in this world and the Hereafter and strive accordingly - [2:201].

(C) Those who sell themselves for the pleasure of God (swt) - [2:207]

If you chose (A) you are destined for the Hell-Fire so reform yourselves. If you chose (B) you are with the majority of those destined for heaven. If you chose (C) you would be in the minority of those destined for Heaven but among the best. You will have the best reward.

The rewards of three general ranks of achievement (in the Hereafter) are described in Chapter 56 verses 7-96 of the Holy Qurán (See also verses 35:32, 39:68-75, 30:14-16, 42:07). The best rank belongs to the foremost doers of good deeds, the Sa-bee-qoon (foremost in faith). They will be the ones close to All-Mighty God[swt]—[56:10-11; See also 35:23; 38:40; 83:28; 3:45; 35:32; 34:37; 23:57-61; 38:45-48, 2:207; 9:72] and thus have the greatest reward. Most believers will want this rank, but only a small percentage will achieve it. The rest of the believers, whose good deeds outweighed their bad deeds, will be placed in the second-best rank that is referred to as belonging to the Companions of The Right Hand (i.e. Dwellers of Heaven)—[101:06-09]; [2:201; 56:27-38]. The ones whose good deeds did not avail them of their bad deeds are referred to as belonging to the Companions of The Left Hand—[56:41-44; 101:06-09; 2:81; 2:[illegible]; 11:106-107] or the dwellers of the Hell-Fire; and most of mankind are disbelievers—[12:103; 12:106; 16:83; 13:01; 26:08; 26:121; 26:158; 26:174; 26:190; See also 8:23; 37:71; 39:71; 36:07; 26:67; 11:40].

Within each of the three general ranks are subrankings—[17:21; 20:75; 6:132; 34:37; 3:163; 46:19]. Although the details of the subrankings are not given, the Qurán does tend to indicate that the Munafaqeen (Muslim hypocrites)—[4:145; See also 3:106-107] and those who followed Pharaoh against Moses[saws]—[40:46; See also 11:97-98; 43:51-56; 27:14; 10:83; 28:40-42] as having the lowest rank (i.e. being placed in the lowest level of the Hell-Fire or having the most severe torment). Perhaps the 7 gates of Hell mentioned in the Qurán refer to these subrankings–[15:44]; each level corresponding to their efforts of evil–[6:131-132; 3:162-163; 46:12-19]. Similarly, there are subrankings in Heaven. For example, the believing fighters (mujahadeen) who answer the call of God to fight in His path have a greater rank than those believers that don't fight–[4:95-96; 9:20; see also 49:15; 9:121]; and among those who fight, the ones who fight when Islam is weak have a greater rank than those who fight when Islam is strong–[57:10; see also 3:172]. The most honourable amongst men, in the eyes of All-Mighty God are the ones with the most taqwa–[49:13; 3:76; see also 2:197]. Commonly translated as God-fearing, taqwa is acting on the remembrance of All-Mighty God in such a way that one guards against earning His displeasure and thus behaves accordingly. Like our pure-hearted father Abraham–[22:78; 37:84; see also 33:40]; whom All-Mighty Allāh took as a friend–[4:125], our beloved seal–[33:40] of the Prophets (Muhammad) and Messenger to all of mankind–[7:158; 34:28; 62:3; 21:107; see also 48:28-29] is described by our Most-Perfect Lord as an excellent role model and of an exalted character for those who look forward to the meeting of their Blessed Lord in the Hereafter–[33:21, see also 60:04-06; 3:68; 16:120-16:123]. It should also be noted that even those who are incorrectly worshipped by man as a means of approach to God or as partner-gods (i.e. Jesus, angels, saints, etc.) have absolutely no power-[17:56; 7:197; 7:194; 46:05; 21:43-44; 10:49; 25:03; See also 2:165-166; 16:20-21; 19:81-82; 2:255; 21:66; 35:14; 45:10], are unaware of the prayers/requests made to them-[46:05, 35:14], and are themselves competing to be close to All-Mighty God-[17:57; 17:55, 17:79; See also 2:253; 6:86]. The Quran says:

> Say (to the disbelievers): "Invoke those whom you presume besides Him (God). They have no power to remove the harm from you nor to modify [it]." Those whom they invoke do seek towards their Lord the means of approach as to who of them is nearer; and they hope for His mercy and fear His punishment. Verily the punishment of your Lord is to be guarded against-[17:56-57; See also 7:194, 7:197; 21:43; 10:49; 25:03; 2:165-166].

Jesus is specifically mentioned as an honored slave of God who has secured a high rank (i.e. placed near All-Mighty God)-[3:45; See also 43:59; 21:26-27; 2:253]. The Quran says:

When the angels said: "O
Maryam, verily Allah gives
you the good tidings of a word
from Him — his name will be
Messiah, Isa (Jesus), son of Maryam,
esteemed in the world and
the Hereafter and of those
placed near — [3:45]".
And they say: "The [Most-]
Merciful has taken a son."
Sacrosanct is He. Nay they (i.e. Jesus and Uzayr)
are servants bestowed honors.
They do not forestall Him in
saying: but they by His
command do act — [21:26-27].
He (Jesus) is naught but a
servant We bestowed favor
on and made him an example
for the Children of Israel — [43:59].
(* David and Solomon have also secured close ranks: — [38:25; 38:40])

Jesus and the honored slaves of All-Mighty
God are never to proud to worship Him — [7:206;
16:49-50; 21:19-20]. Any power given to them is given to
them as servants of God not as equals to God — [illegible]

The Covenant: Our Weakness and God's Mercy

It will be surprising for many to learn, and All-Mighty God speaks the truth-[18:29; 3:95; 3:108; 22:04; 6:146], that mankind (i.e. the progeny of the children of Adam) not only previously testified that All-Mighty Allah is our only Lord-[7:172-173; 36:60-61; See also 57:08], but mankind (i.e. our early forefathers on our behalf, perhaps; or some suggest we all did while in the loins of Adam but forgot) also accepted what is referred to as the "Amanah" (Trust)-[33:72; See also 57:08 (5:7); 8:27; 7:102]:

> We indeed offered the Amanah (i.e. trust/covenant) to the heavens and the earth and the mountains, but they declined to carry it and shirked it; but man bore it. Verily he is unjust and ignorant-[33:72; See also 57:08; 8:27; 2:30].
> No indeed. He (man) has not carried out what He (God) commanded him-[80:23].
> And We did not find in most of them (adherence to) the covenant, but We found most of them indeed disobedient-[7:102].

The details aren't given, but this "Trust" seems to have ultimately manifested into mankind being tested by God to see who obeys His commandments the best, which translates into good deeds. Although it may sound strange or unfair to be bound to a covenant that we did not directly participate in (or remember participating in), All-Mighty God makes the rules; we are bound to the trust/covenant not unlike the descendants of the Children of Israel (i.e. the Jews) are bound to the covenant their early forefathers made. And although their may be a renewal or modifications made to previous covenants after many generations (i.e. by the way of prophets), worshipping and obedience to the Only One Mighty God has never changed. It's interesting to note that other forms of creation declined the offer to accept this "Trust", presumably, because of fear of not being able to keep this "Trust" – [33:72, see also 17:44; 22:18; 41:11; 24:41; 34:10]. Their fear was warranted. Fortunately, despite wronging ourselves for ignorantly agreeing to a "Trust" we didn't have the firm will power to keep (i.e. we all sin – [16:61; 24:21; 35:45; see also 20:115; 53:32; 2:187; 7:102]), it's obvious our Most-Merciful God wants us to succeed – [4:31; 39:33-35; 53:32; 46:16; 29:07; 42:20; 42:34; 40:07-09; 42:05; 4:28 33:43; 25:70-71; 16:106; see also 9:71; 9:102-105; 7:171]. According to the Qurán preserved by our forefathers All-Mighty God says:

> If you avoid the major sins
> of what you are prohibited from,
> We shall efface from you your (minor)
> sins and shall admit you into
> a noble place of admittance (i.e.
> Paradise) – [4:31; see also 53:32; 46:16].

> And those who believe and do the good deeds, We shall surely efface from their sins and surely reward them for the best of what they use to do—[29:07].

The next verse is even more encouraging because it implies that the major sins can also be forgiven:

> That Allah may remit for them (God-fearing) the worst of what they did and reward them their due for the best of what they use to do—[39:35; See also 39:53-54]; [41:27].

Perhaps, this is what All-Mighty God means when He says He created mankind to have mercy on them—[11:119; see also 20:115-124]; and indeed, He is the Most-Merciful of those who show mercy.

Like our father Adam who lacked the firm will-power to stay away from the forbidden tree and later repented—[20:115-122; 2:35-39; 7:11-25], or Jonah, who repented—[21:87] after being punished by his Lord for losing patience—[37:139-148; 21:87-88; 68:48], or many other prominent believers—[38:30-35; 38:24-25; 38:44; 47:19; 40:55; 11:75; see also 94:2-3; 11:46-48; 12:91-92], our Lord wants to have mercy on and forgive the believing doers of good of their sins—[17:25; 34:04; 35:07; 36:11; 4:26-27, 19:58-60, 40:07; 20:22; 42:02; 46:15-16; 39:35; 48:02; 42:05; 60:12; 64:09; 48:29; 25:69-71; 7:153; 2:153], and multiply their good deeds—[6:160; 4:173; 42:23; 2:261; 4:40; 24:38; 27:89; 10:26; 28:84; 34:37; 64:17; 16:97; 35:30] so we can enter into Heaven:

The Day He (Allah) will gather you for the Day of Gathering (i.e. Day of Judgement). That will be the day of mutual gain and loss. And whoever believes and does good (i.e. good deeds) He will efface from him his sins and will admit him in gardens flowing below the rivers (i.e. Heaven); abiding therein for ever. That is the success most magnificent—[64:09]. Those who disbelieve they shall have a punishment very severe (i.e. Hell). And those who believe and do the good deeds they shall have forgiveness and a reward very great (i.e. Heaven)—[35:07]. Whoever comes up with a good deed shall have ten the like of it; and whoever comes up with a bad deed shall not be requited except with its equivalent, and they shall not be wronged—[6:160; See also 4:40]

Our Most-Merciful Lord[swt] even has the angels[as] asking for our forgiveness-[40:07, 42:05] and is so merciful that He[swt] exchanges the sins of an idol worshipper who repents and becomes a Muslim into good deeds-[25:69-71; see also 7:152-153]. Our Lord[swt] is Most-Generous, full of Love-[85:14; see also 19:96], but He[swt] expects us to make an acceptable effort-[17:19; see also 46:13; 79:37-41; 53:39-41; 7:161-162; 7:170; 8:53; 7:161-166]; and we need His[swt] help every step of the way-[81:28-29; see also 12:53; 10:09; 11:119; 14:27; 47:17; 74:56]:

> Allah[swt] wants to make clear to you and to guide you to the ways of those before you (i.e. the pious) and to forgive you; and Allah[swt] is [All-]Knowing, [All-]Wise. And Allah[swt] wants to forgive you but there want those who follow the desires that you bend an enormous bending. Allah[swt] wants to make light on you (i.e. the rules of God[swt]); for man has been created weak (i.e. against desires and temptations)-[4:26-28].
> And those who receive guidance He[swt] increases them in guidance and

gives them their piety—[47:17]. Verily, those who say: "Our Lord is Allah" then remain upright no fear will be on them nor will they grieve—[46:13]. And you may not will (to be upright) except that there wills Allah, Lord of all beings—[81:28-29]. Verily those who believe and do good deeds, their Lord guides them through their faith. There will flow below them the rivers in the Gardens of Bliss (i.e. Heaven)—[10:09].

As mentioned earlier, an acceptable effort to avoid the Hell-fire and enter into Heaven means that ones good deeds aren't overwhelmed by ones bad deeds that All-Mighty God doesn't forgive directly or pardon indirectly (i.e. by allowing the intercession of others)—[101:06-11; 99:06-08; 2:81; 7:08-09; 23:101-104; 2:255]. The following verses are similar to an earlier verse but presented differently:

On the Day (i.e. The Day of Judgement) every individual will come arguing for himself; and fully paid will be each individual for what it wrought and they will not be wronged—[16:111]. And that there is not for man aught but what he strives for. And that his effort shall be looked into. Then he will be requited for it the fullest requital—[53:39-41]. And that to your Lord[SWT] is the final destination—[53:42]. And the weighing on that Day (i.e. The Day of Judgement) is true. Then as to those whose scales become heavy (with good deeds) they would be the ones attaining success (ie. Heaven). And as to those whose scales (of good deeds) became light, they would be those who would have lost themselves (i.e. entering into Hell), because they had been to Our[SWT] revelations doing wrong—[7:08-09]. There will scorch their faces the fire and they in there will frown in despair—[23:104-101].

Making an Acceptable Effort

All-Mighty God[SWT] Knows and specifically tells us that He[SWT] has created man weak—[4:28; See also 50:16; 8:46], impatient—[70:19-20], and in hardship—[90:04]. We are prone to transgress—[46:6-7] and desire to sin—[75:05; see also 12:53; 50:16-18]. We are also told we are rash—[17:11; 21:37], worry alot—[70:20; 41:49], are argumentive—[18:54], greedy—[70:21; 17:100; see also 4:128], and have many other characteristics that can doom us to failure—[102:1-2; 89:20; 100:04; 42:27; 74:12-15]. All-Mighty God[SWT] tells us if He[SWT] were to punish mankind for their wrong-doings none of us would be spared—[16:61; 35:45; see also 24:21; 7:100; 18:58; 20:129]; so none of us should ascribe purity to ourselves—[53:32, see also 17:25, 24:21]. All-Mighty God[SWT] tells us to fear Him[SWT] the best we can—[64:16; see also 36:11] and to at least stay away from intentionally—[4:17-18] committing the major sins—[53:32; 4:31]; and indeed He[SWT] pardons much—[42:30; 13:06; 42:24; see also 49:14]:

> And indeed We[SWT] have created man and We[SWT] know wherewith there tempts him his self; and We[SWT] are nearer to him than the jugular vein—[50:16]. Allah[SWT] intends to make light (i.e. rules of God[SWT]) on you; for man has been created weak—[4:28; see also 8:66]. We have indeed created man in hardship—[90:04]. And were Allah[SWT] to punish men for their wrong-doing He[SWT] would not leave on it any moving creature; but He[SWT] puts them off till a term

specified. So when their term comes they cannot delay [it] an hour nor can they advance [it] – [16:61]. So beware (i.e. fear) of Allah[SWT] as much as you are able to; listen and obey; and spend for the good of yourselves (i.e. with the Hereafter in mind) – [64:16]. Those who refrain from the enormities of sin and adulteries except the trivilaites, Verily your Lord[SWT] is All-Abounding in forgiveness. He is Best Aware of you when He[SWT] created you from the earth and when you were embryos in the wombs of your mothers. So declare not purity about yourselves. He[SWT] is Best Aware of anyone who is on his guard (i.e. God-fearing) – [53:32]. And whatever afflicts you of misfortune that is due to what your hands acquire; and He[SWT] forgives a lot – [42:30]. Indeed man does transgress, because he thinks he is in no need – [96:06-07]. And prays for the evil like his praying for the good; for man is rash – [17:11]. And indeed We[SWT] have elucidated in this Qurán for man every kind of similies; but man is in most matters argumentive – [18:54]. Nay, but man desires to commit sin onward – [75:05]. 24

The hard part isn't for All-Merciful Allāh to forgive us for our previous sins—[4:110; 8:38; 4:106; 2:160; 4:145-146]; the hard part is for us to stay on the straight path after He forgives us—[20:82; 46:13; 8:38; 4:137; 4:91; 25:71; 4:146; 25:70-71]:

And whoever does an evil or wrongs himself and then seeks forgiveness of Allāh will find Allāh [Most] Forgiving, Merciful—[4:110]. And verily I am Oft-Forgiving to those who repent and return and believe and act rightly, then remain on the right way—[20:82]. Verily, those who say: "Our Lord is Allāh" then remain upright, no fear will be on them nor will they grieve—[46:13]. Verily those who disbelieve after their having believed, and then they increase in disbelief, never will be accepted their repentance; and they are the ones gone astray—[4:90-91]. Verily Allāh wrongs not man whatsoever; but men to themselves do wrong—[10:44]. Your Lord Knows best what is in yourselves. If you are righteous, then He indeed is for the oft-returning penitents, Forgiving—[17:25].

All-Mighty God[swt] tells those who have transgressed their souls not to despair from the mercy of their All-Mighty Lord[swt], for He[swt] forgives sins altogether—[39:53-54; 15:56; 12:87; See also 8:38; 28:67; 4:145-146], but, to sincerely reform themselves before their appointed time—[63:11], when the threshold of ones final death is at hand—[4:18; See also 10:90-91; 39:53-55; 8:53; 10:51-52; 10:98; 40:84-85] and to strive on:

> Say (O Muhammad[saws] to mankind): "O My[swt] servants (i.e. God's[swt] (mankind) servants) who have transgressed against themselves, be not in despair of the mercy of Allah[swt]. Verily, Allah[swt] forgives the sins altogether. Verily He is the [Most-] Forgiving, the Merciful. And turn in repentance to your Lord[swt] and surrender to Him[swt] before that there comes to you the punishment; then you will not be helped—[39:53-54] see also 15:56; 12:87]. Say to those who disbelieve, if they desist they will be forgiven for what has been past. But if they revert, then there already has gone by the practice with ancients—[8:38] 4:145-146; 3:91]. 'Forgiveness is not for those who do the evil deeds till when there appears death to anyone of them he says:

"I repent now"; nor for those who die while they are unbelievers. Such people, We[SWT] have ready for them an agonizing punishment-[4:18]. And Allah[SWT] will not defer anyone when there comes his appointed time. And Allah[SWT] is [All-] Aware of what you do-[63:11].

Man will ultimately get what he strives for and will not be dealt with unjustly-[21:47; 2:286; 3:161; 10:47; 10:54]; and whoever strives, he strives for himself, for God[SWT] is not in need of us or our striving-[29:06; 20:15; 76:22; 79:35-41; 39:35; 29:06-07; 20:82; 25:71; See also 33:70-71; 2:160]. On the Day of Judgement every individual will be arguing to God[SWT] on his own behalf-[16:111] and All-Mighty God[SWT] will reward our efforts with fairness and justice-[10:04]:

On the day (i.e. Day of Judgement) every individual will come arguing for himself; and fully paid will be each individual what it wrought and they will not be wronged-[16:111].

... And the Day the Hour shall take place... And you will see every people down on their knees. Every people will be called to their book (of deeds). Today you will be requited for what you used to do. This book (i.e. the record of deeds) of Ours[SWT] speaks about you with truth. Indeed We[SWT] had been transcribing all that you used to do. So as to those who believe and do the good deeds, their Lord[SWT] will admit them to His[SWT] Mercy. That will be the success most conspicuous. And as for those who disbelieved... clear to them will be the evils of what they did; and there will encircle them what they used to mock at. And it will be said: "Today We[SWT] forget you as you did forget the meeting of this day of yours. And your abode is the fire, and you shall not have any helper — [45:27-34].

Good Deeds in Brief

These tests, to see who of us are best in good deeds, that we are rewarded for and determines our final rank in the Hereafter have numerous forms. Several examples with additional commentary are given below. Further details are given in corresponding chapters.

- Monotheism: All good deeds hang on the tree of monotheism. There is absolutely no compromise! Those who die their final death worshipping other than Allāh are not forgiven - [4:48; 4:116; See also 45:23; 18:36-42; 17:22; 47:34], and their good deeds are rendered useless on the Day of Judgement - [9:17; 47:08-09; 47:01; 18:102-106; 14:18; See also 39:64-65; 39:15; 18:110; 25:23; 35:08; 39:45; 45:10; 6:87-88; 17:39; 24:39]. (See section on monotheism)

- Obedience: The tree of (ones claim to) monotheism - which the fruits of all good deeds hang - is only as strong as it's roots of obedience. Once an order is decreed by All-Mighty God, mankind has no option except to obey - [33:36; See also 08:20; 47:33-34; 39:13; 21:108; 22:01; 72:23] or face the prospect of losing all of ones good deeds - [47:33-34], and being thrown into Hell - [4:14; 6:15; See also 47:26-28; 10:15]. (See section on obedience.)

- Remembrance: We are told to remember All-Mighty God[SWT] within ourselves with humility and fear-[7:205]; and to remember Him[SWT] abundantly and intensely-[33:41; 2:200; see also 20:42], devoting ourselves in true devotion-[73:08], so He[SWT] will remember us-[2:152; 9:67], and that we may be successful-[62:10; 8:45]. Remember Him[SWT] for He[SWT] has guided us-[2:198]; and don't forget Him[SWT] or He[SWT] will forget us-[32:14; 45:34] and make us forget ourselves-[59:19; see also 7:51; 9:67]. (See section on Remembrance)

- Taqwa: The most honourable amongst mankind in the sight of All-Mighty God[SWT] is the one who has the most taqwa-[49:13; 3:76; See also 2:197; 7:26-27]. Commonly translated as God[SWT]-fearing, taqwa is acting on the remembrance of the One and Only God[SWT] (Allah[SWT]) in such a way that it guards against earning His[SWT] displeasure and thus one behaves accordingly and is rendered obedient. The pious are God-fearing; those that are mindful of God[SWT]-[2:189].

- Gratitude: Expressing gratitude to our Lord[SWT] is an often repeated commandment-[39:66; 2:172; 16:114] and is described as wisdom-[31:12; See also 2:269], and pleasing-[39:07] to All-Mighty God[SWT].

- **<u>Accepting The Quránic Revelation</u>:** All-Mighty God[swt] has sent down the best speech as a Book (i.e. Qurán)-[39:23, see also 15:87] to guide mankind-[42:52; 4:174; 5:15; 64:8; 3:138]. The Qurán is such that no one, but, All-Mighty God[swt] could have created it-[10:37]. God[swt] asks, if the disbelievers dont believe in the Qurán, then in what discourse will they believe-[77:50; 45:06; see also 7:185]? All-Mighty God[swt] renders vain the deeds of those who hate the Quránic revelation-[47:08-09].

- **<u>Calling Others to All-Mighty God[swt] and The People of The Book (i.e. Jews, Christians, etc.)</u>:** Among the best of speeches is the calling of others to All-Mighty God[swt] by righteous Muslims-[41:33]. We are told to call to the way of our Lord[swt] with wisdom-[16:125] and to also remind the believers, for reminding is beneficial-[51:55; see also 22:24]. All-Mighty God[swt] refers to the people of book (i.e Jews, Christians, etc.) who don't accept Islam as the worst of creatures-[98:06; see also 45:08-10; 58:05]. Those who disbelieve and hinder the people from the path of All-Mighty God[swt] and die in that state will not be forgiven-[47:34; 8:36] and their good deeds will be in vain-[47:01; see also 24:39].

- **Jihad:** The willingness to fight for All-Mighty God[swt] can be a test in of itself–[2:216; 47:30; 9:38-39; 3:142; 9:16; 4:77; 3:140; 9:44-49; 3:154; 3:166; 47:20]. Sometimes God[swt] would have to threaten the Muslims to get them to fight–[9:38-39]. The believers are told not to be afraid of the blame of the blamers–[5:54]; and fear Allah[swt] more than the disbelievers–[4:77; 9:13; see also 8:05-06], and fight in His[swt] way so that we may attain success–[5:35; see also 47:04; 62:10-11]. Angering and inflicting harm on the enemies of God[swt] will count as a good deed–[9:120-121]. Believing fighters have a greater rank in the eyes of Allah[swt] than believers who don't fight–[4:95-96; 9:20; see also 49:15; 9:121]; and those who fight when Islam is weak have a greater rank than those who wait to fight until Islam is strong–[57:10; see also 2:172]. The believers are to inspire the Muslims to fight–[4:84; 8:65].

- **Not Dividing Into Religious Sects:** All-Mighty God[swt] makes clear He[swt] doesn't like those who divide their religion into sects; each sect happy with the differences that set them apart from each other–[23:52-53; 6:159; 3:103; 30:32; 3:105; 42:13-14; see also 21:92-93]. All-Mighty God[swt] likes when the believers fight as one unified structure–[61:04] and tells us to obey Him[swt] and not to wrangle amongst ourselves or else we will lose "heart" and "spirit"–[8:46; see also 8:01; 8:73; 3:152]. Believers are told to speak using the best of words, for Satan is trying to sow conflict amongst us—[17:53]. Believers are not to kill other believers except by the way of justice—[2:178] or by mistake—[4:92], and perhaps during the intervention of 2 different warring parties of believers, siding with the truth—[49:09-10]. The believers are brothers—[49:10] and are merciful among each other, and severe against the disbelievers—[49:10]. We are told to refrain from spying and backbiting, as well as from most surmising—[49:12]. I ask All-Mighty God[SWT] to unite the hearts of the believers as He[SWT] did for our brethren in the past—[8:63; see also 11:118-119].

- Asking for Forgiveness and Forgiving Others: Our Most-Beautiful Lord[SWT] refers to Himself[SWT] as the Forgiving, Loving God[SWT]—[85:14; see also 15:49; 11:90; 11:05; 2:199; 8:38] and loves those who repent—[2:222]. We are also told to forgive one another—[3:134; see also 12:92] and reminded that we would want to be forgiven—[24:22; see also 42:43]. The reward for those who do good deeds is forgiveness—[3:135-136].

- **Patience During Tests / Relying on Allah[SWT]:** Whether one is a believer or a disbeliever God[SWT] can test us. A test of hardship or punishment may serve as a vehicle for repentance and return to their Most-Merciful Lord[SWT]—[9:126; 32:21; 23:76; 68:17-33; 52:47; 46:27; 43:48; 7:168-167; 17:59-60; 23:75-77; 30:41; 39:24-26; 41:15-17; 7:167-168]. Again, believing doesn't exempt us from tests of hardships—[8:25; 29:02-03]. All-Mighty God[SWT] can test us with fear, hunger, loss of life, fluctuations in wealth, family members, etc.—[2:155; 2:214; 3:186; 64:14-15; 8:28; 47:31; See also 11:9-11; 25:20; 72:16-17; 57:23; 7:163; 29:02]. No calamity befalls anyone without the permission of All-Mighty God[SWT]—[64:11; See also 12:21]. During adversity All-Mighty God[SWT] instructs us to seek help with patience and prayer, relying on Him[SWT]—[14:12, See also 12:67; 13:22; 65:03; 2:156-157], and putting our trust in Him[SWT]—[3:122; 12:122; 25:58; 33:03]. He[SWT] tells us it's hard to implement His[SWT] instructions unless one is humble—[2:45]; and He[SWT] does not burden anyone beyond their capacity—[2:286; 6:152; 7:42; 23:62; 65:07]. Whoever fears All-Mighty God[SWT] and keeps their duty to Him, He[SWT] will make a way out of any difficulty and provide from sources never expected—[65:02-04; 3:120; 3:125; 7:96; 8:29]. Be patient, for along every hardship is relief—[94:05-06].

- <u>Avoiding Usury, Gambling, and Alcohol</u>: Usury or interest is such an evil sin All-Mighty Allah[SWT] declares war on those who take usury/interest and will place them in Hell if they don't stop—[2:275-280]. All-Mighty God[SWT] warns those who try to compare interest to trading; Allah[SWT] permits trading and forbids interest—[2:275; see also 3:130; 4:161; 30:39]. Gambling and alcohol should also be avoided. Satan uses gambling and alcohol as a way to excite enmity and hatred, and hinder men from the rememebrance of their All-Praiseworthy Lord—[5:90-92].

- <u>Giving Charity</u>: One of the marks of a believer is charity—[2:177; 76:08-11; 23:04; 64:16-18; 2:277]. Satan instills the fear of poverty to those who give charity—[2:268] whereas God[SWT] assures the believers He[SWT] will augment what is given in charity—[2:276; 57:11; 57:18; 64:17; 30:39; see also 63:10; 2:245]; and promises the givers of charity forgiveness—[2:268-271; see also 9:102-105].

- <u>Performing The Prayers of Worship (Salat)</u>: The obligatory ritual prayers (salat) are one of the marks of the righteous God[SWT] fearing believers - [2:03; 2:177; 5:55; 13:22; 22:41; 24:37; 27:03; 31:04; 42:38; 23:01-02]. Our Most-Merciful Lord[SWT] tells us that the prayers of worship (salat) help prevent us from commiting bad deeds as well as erase the bad deeds that are committed - [11:114; 29:45] Those who scorn the worship of All-Mighty God[SWT] will enter into Hell humiliated - [40:60; 4:173; 68:42-43].

- <u>Keeping Oaths, Covenants, Trusts, and Contracts</u>: All-Mighty God[SWT] makes clear the importance of Keeping oaths, covenants, trusts, and contracts - [13:25; 6:152; 13:20; 5:01; 2:27; 23:08; 48:10; 70:32; 4:58; 2:177; 8:27; 3:75-76]. Those who sell Gods[SWT] covenant for worldy desires will have no portion in the Hereafter and will be punished severely - [3:77].

- Guarding Against Satan (Shayton): All-Mighty God[swt] has given Satan permission to test mankind-[34:21; 17:64; See also 14:22, 7:11-18; 59:16; 15:42; 17:61-65] to know who really believes in the Hereafter from the one who is in doubt about it-[34:21; See also 4:120; 59:16]. We are told Satan will lead most of us astray-[36:60-62; 12:103; 2:208; 34:20; 47:25]. And most of mankind are disbelievers-[12:103; 12:106; 16:83; 13:01; 26:08; 26:121; 26:158; 26:174; 26:190; See also 8:23; 17:71; 39:71; 36:07; 26:67; 11:40].

- Not Being Deceived by The Ornaments of Life: We are warned by All-Mighty God[swt] that this worldy life with all of its adornments is temporary and just part of His[swt] Test; a delight of delusion, enjoyment of deception, a diversion of fun and games, and not to be deceived by them-[57:20; 3:185; 6:32; 47:36; 29:64; 18:07; 11:07; 3:14; 18:46]. Yet, despite these warnings, God[swt] states man prefers this worldy life-[76:27; 87:16; 75:20] thats fleeting-[79:46; 13:26]; leaving aside the hereafter-[75:21; 76:27], and won't be concerned until seeing the punishment--[102:01-08; 40:84-85; 26:201; 89:23-24; 78:40; 82:06; 74:46-47]. Those who transgress and prefer the worldly life will dwell in Hell-[79:37-39; 17:18]; their good deeds are rendered useless-[18:28]; and most of mankind are disbelievers-[12:103; 12:106].

- <u>Taking Heed</u>: The Holy Qurán is full of verses depicting the future statements of the dwellers of the Hell-Fire expressing regret for not taking heed-67:07-11; See also 25:27; 33:66; 21:97; 39:71; 6:31; 23:76-77], asking for a second chance-[40:11; 63:10-11; See also 42:44; 32:12; 14:14; 23:103-108; 37:167-169; 26:96-102; 6:27-28; 26:203], blaming one another for being lead astray-[34:31-33; 37:27-34; 40:47-50; 41:29; 50:24-30; 2:166-167; 43:67; 38:59-64; 25:28-29; 33:67-68]; even blaming All-Mighty God[SWT] Himself-[43:20; See also 7:16-18; 39:57], and asking to die because of the severe torment-[43:72-78; 35:36-37; 25:12-14; See also 40:49-50; 44:43-50; 35:36; 32:20; 14:49-50; 21:39-40; 22:19-22; 11:106; 6:93; 14:16-17]. At that time, All-Mighty God's[SWT] aversion to them will be made clear-[40:10; See also 40:49-50; 32:20]. All-Mighty God[SWT] makes clear that predestiny, fatalism, or other arguments won't be accepted-[43:20; See also 43:76; 39:57; 7:173; 6:148-149; 7:179; 10:99-101; 16:35-36]; and there is no second chance after one dies their final death-[63:10-11; 50:28-30; 2:161-162; 4:18; 7:53; See also 74:42-47; 39:56-59; 6:27-28]. And most of mankind are disbelievers-[12:103; 12:106].

- <u>Making an Acceptable Effort</u>: Just like in this world, where one has to make an effort to accomplish ones goal/ambitions-[11:15-16; 2:202], one has to make a similiar effort to be successful in the Hereafter-[17:19-21; 46:19; 6:132; 20:75]. One has to find a balance that ideally emphasizes the Hereafter, but at the very least, doesn't neglect the Hereafter—[11:15-16; See also 2:200-202; 18:46; 2:14]. As for those who didn't make an acceptable effort, if any effort at all, All-Mighty God[SWT] informs them that they were given their appointed portion of good things in the worldly life and now its time for recompense—Hell—[17:18]. And most of mankind are disbelievers—[12:103; 12:106].

- <u>Not Taking The Disbelievers as Friends</u>: All-Mighty God[SWT] tells the believers not to take the disbelievers (Jews, Christians, Polytheists, and Hypocrites) as friends except under certain circumstances and with some exceptions—[3:28; 4:89-90; 60:08-09; 9:23-24; 29:08; 5:05; 5:51; 4:144; 3:118; 60:13; 45:19; 58:14-16; 58:22; 60:1-2; 5:57]. Obviously, Muslims should not take as friends those who oppose/fight Islam—[58:22; 60:1-2; 5:57]. After that, by the Mercy of All-Mighty God[SWT], He does seem to allow exceptions—[60:08-09; 4:89-90; 5:05; 29:08]. If these exceptions weren't later abrogated by verses like 9:23-24, that are said to be some of the last verses revealed (or perhaps more accurately are in the last chapter revealed), then in such relationships it is up to the Muslim not to be influenced to disobey God's[SWT] commands—[29:08; 6:121; See also 9:31; 11:113; 9:23-24]. All-Mighty God[SWT] warns us that the disbelievers won't fail to or try to corrupt us or confuse us or cause us mischief—[3:18; See also 5:49; 11:113]. Some disbelievers knowingly try to deceive us—[3:100; 5:69; 4:44; 6:116; 6:153; 2:109; 2:120; 2:145; 18:28], but, others are ignorant and sincerely believe in the falsehood they were taught—[9:30; 18:04; 5:73; 5:17; 10:66; 9:36; 11:109; 22:8-10]. The believers are reminded that men will lie about their Lord[SWT]—[72:03-04]. And most of mankind are disbelievers—[12:103; 12:106].

- **<u>Earning The Love of All-Mighty God[SWT]</u>:** Our Beautiful Lord[SWT] describes Himself[SWT] as a Loving God[SWT]—[85:14]; and prophets have delivered this message to their people—[11:89-90]. Although His[SWT] Mercy encompasses all of mankind—[7:156; 6:12; 6:54; see also 11:119], His[SWT] Love appears to be conditional on ones obedience—[3:31; See also 19:96; 5:54]. After that, All-Mighty God[SWT] chooses whom He[SWT] pleases to cast His[SWT] Love upon, as He[SWT] did upon Moses[SAWS], when Moses[SAWS] was reared under God's[SWT] Eyes—[20:39].

- **<u>Avoiding Gods[SWT] Hatred/Anger</u>:** All-Mighty God[SWT] does not like those who reject faith—[40:10-12]. And although God[SWT] does not like the disbelievers (or traits of disbelievers)—[3:32; 35:39; 7:55; 4:107; 30:45; See also 16:23; 7:55; 7:51; 7:31; 17:37-38; 22:38; 31:18; 40:35; 17:83], His[SWT] Mercy encompasses all of mankind—[7:156]. That is, All-Mighty God[SWT] tells us He[SWT] has prescribed Mercy upon Himself—[6:12; 6:54; See also 11:119] allowing the disbelievers respite to either eventually take heed–[35:37; 2:160; 7:182-183; 7:168-169] or enjoy themselves as disbelievers (as God[SWT] wills)–[17:18; 42:20; 42:36; 68:44-45] until they die, when God's[SWT] Mercy will be removed (i.e. they will be placed in the Hell-Fire)–[46:20; 2:178; 2:161-162; 18:58; 9:85; 2:126; 42:20; 11:15-16; 17:18; 18:100-101; 4:56; 45:34-35; 14:42; 3:91; 16:84-85]. The believers are told not to ask forgiveness for those who have died as disbelievers–[9:113; 9:84; 9:80; See also 4:18]. God[SWT] is who He[SWT] is, and does as He[SWT] pleases–[85:16; 22:14; 22:18; 22:18; See also 2:253; 21:23]. And most of mankind are disbelievers–[12:103; 12:106].

- Loving God[SWT]: The believers love All-Mighty God[SWT] more than the disbelievers love their invented gods–[2:165]. The believers can prove their love for All-Mighty God[SWT] by obeying Him[SWT] and His[SWT] Messengers[SAWS]–[3:31].

- Fearing God[SWT]: All-Mighty God[SWT] wants to be feared–[22:35; 23:57-60; 2:197; 2:194; 2:196; 2:231; 5:108; 10:31; 5:100; 39:16; 2:40; 33:33; 2:235; 2:278; 2:281; 2:282; 3:102; 22:35; 2:180; 4:131; 5:02; 5:03; 5:08; 5:35]. In fact, the most honourable amongst mankind in the eyes of All-Mighty God[SWT] is the most God[SWT]-fearing (Taqwa)–[49:13; 3:76; See also 2:197]; and it is considered the best attire one can wear–[7:26-27].

Summary and Final Comments

The aforementioned examples are all considered good deeds, and All-Mighty God[swt] is appreciative of – [76:22; 2:158] and loves the doers of good (Muh-see-neen) – [3:134; 3:148; 2:195]. Again, the most honourable amongst us in the sight of All-Mighty Allah[swt] is the one who has the most taqwa[God-fearing] – [49:13; 3:76; see also 2:197 7:26-27]. All-Mighty God[swt] says:

> O mankind, indeed We[swt] have created you from a male and a female and have made you peoples and tribes that you may know one another. Verily, the most honourable in the sight of Allah is the one most God-fearing (i.e. righteous, pious). Verily Allah[swt] is Knowing, Aware – [49:13, see also 3:76; 2:197].

Taqwa is acting on the remembrance of All-Mighty God[swt] in such a way that it guards one against earning His[swt] displeasure and thus one behaves accordingly. Commonly understood as God[swt]-fearing/pious/righteous, it is taqwa that couples the remembrance of All-Mighty God[swt] – [29:45; 8:45] with action (i.e. obedience);

and is thus a powerful prescription for success: God's Love — [3:31] and Mercy — [3:132]. Prophet Muhammad is described by our Most-Perfect Lord as a good example and of an exalted character for those who look forward to the meeting of their Blessed Lord in the Hereafter — [33:21; see also 60:04-06; 2:62; 16:120; 16:123; 37:84; 33:40].

So, in summary, it seems that since mankind lacked the firm will-power to steadfastly uphold their covenant to obey all of God's commandments over our desires and other external influences, All-Mighty God has mercy on us by lowering the standard to enter into Heaven and avoid Hell by telling us to at least make sure our good deeds aren't overwhelmed by our bad deeds. After that, the more good deeds one does relative to their bad deeds, the greater the rank in Heaven. Conversely, those whose bad deeds overwhelm their good deeds will have a rank in Hell that corresponds to the amount of evil they acquired by their own hands. In other words, one's final rank in the Hereafter — in the shadow of All-Mighty God's Mercy, Grace, and Forgiveness — appears to be determined by the net weight of ones good deeds (i.e. the accepted and potentially multiplied good deeds) relative to the weight of ones bad deeds (i.e. the bad deeds that are not forgiven)—[101:06-09; 23:102-103; 2:81; See also 4:85; 24:21; 06:08; 33:32; 17:19-21; 20:75; 6:132; 34:37; 3:162-165; 46:19; 7:08-09; 27:89; 29:12-13; 25:70; 35:69; 16:25; 16:88]. No one will be dealt with unjustly—[36:54; 21:47; 3:161; 10:47; 10:54]. If one is looking for honor, power, and prestige it can be found with the Lord of Honor and Power—All-Mighty Allah[SWT]—[37:180; 35:10; 63:08; 10:65; 18:44; 22:18]. So glorify the praises of your Lord[SWT] and be of those who prostrate themselves and worship until death—[15:98-99].

Ending With a Prayer

O our Most-Glorious Lord[SWT], fasten our hearts with strength, determination, and sincerity when we say, "our prayers (salat), our sacrifice, our living and our dying are for Allah[SWT], the Lord[SWT] of all beings—[6:162]." Please forgive us for our past and future sins—[48:01-02] by Your[SWT] Mercy, multiply our good deeds by Your[SWT] Generosity, guide and maintain us firmly on the straight path by Your[SWT] Power, and enter us into the highest part of Paradise by Your[SWT] Grace. ... Ameen!

Nidal M. Hasan, SoA

"By the time. Verily, man is in loss. Except those who believe and do good deeds—[103:1-3]... theirs shall be the Gardens of Firdaus (Paradise) in entertainment, abiding therein forever—[18:107-108]."

"... the servants of Allāh, the select ones, ... will be honoured in the gardens of bliss—[37:40-61]... They will be given to drink of a nectar kept sealed. The sealing thereof is of musk; and for this, let there strive those who want to strive—[83:22-26]."

We should never idolize villains nor fear the. We should understand them and study them to educate ourselves. Knowledge is power and power over those who dispense fear is far greater than anything they can throw at us. To understand the past is to understand the future. Imagine if we knew the signs of what causes behavior like this. We could prevent so much crime if we just faced our fears and learned from the monsters.

In the end this book is published so many may study Nidal Hasan's manifesto. It's a way to allow many people to see his writings in a safe way.

If you've read to the end and have any questions or want a signed copy of any of my books email me at andrewmcmurphyauthor@gmail.com

www.ingramcontent.com/pod-product-compliance
Lightning Source LLC
LaVergne TN
LVHW050347160826
845677LV00014B/3829

* 9 7 9 8 3 7 1 8 8 3 1 2 4 *